8

D1072516

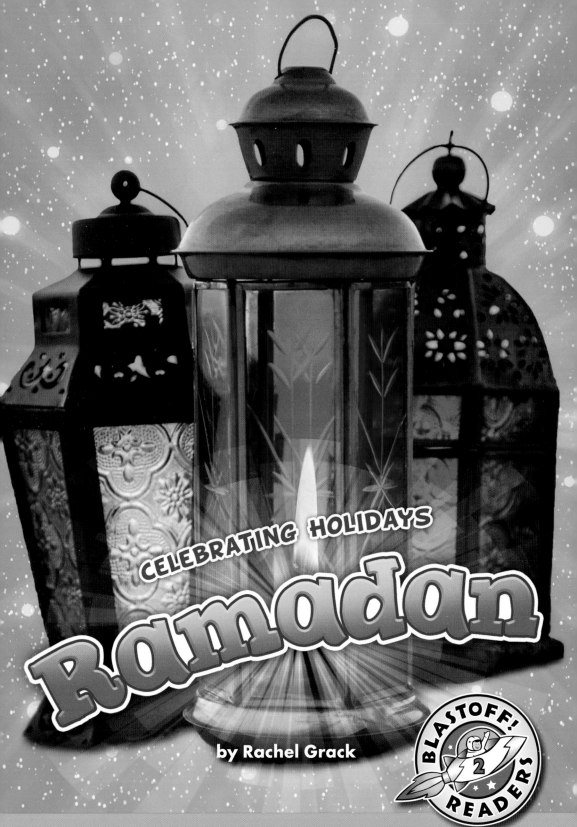

CELEBRATING HOLIDAYS

Ramadan

by Rachel Grack

BLASTOFF!
2
READERS

BELLWETHER MEDIA · MINNEAPOLIS, MN

Note to Librarians, Teachers, and Parents:

Blastoff! Readers are carefully developed by literacy experts and combine standards-based content with developmentally appropriate text.

Level 1 provides the most support through repetition of high-frequency words, light text, predictable sentence patterns, and strong visual support.

Level 2 offers early readers a bit more challenge through varied simple sentences, increased text load, and less repetition of high-frequency words.

Level 3 advances early-fluent readers toward fluency through increased text and concept load, less reliance on visuals, longer sentences, and more literary language.

Level 4 builds reading stamina by providing more text per page, increased use of punctuation, greater variation in sentence patterns, and increasingly challenging vocabulary.

Level 5 encourages children to move from "learning to read" to "reading to learn" by providing even more text, varied writing styles, and less familiar topics.

Whichever book is right for your reader, Blastoff! Readers are the perfect books to build confidence and encourage a love of reading that will last a lifetime!

This edition first published in 2017 by Bellwether Media, Inc.

No part of this publication may be reproduced in whole or in part without written permission of the publisher. For information regarding permission, write to Bellwether Media, Inc., Attention: Permissions Department, 5357 Penn Avenue South, Minneapolis, MN 55419.

Library of Congress Cataloging-in-Publication Data

Names: Koestler-Grack, Rachel A., 1973-, author.
Title: Ramadan / by Rachel Grack.
Description: Minneapolis, MN : Bellwether Media, Inc., 2017. | Series: Blastoff! Readers: Celebrating Holidays | Includes bibliographical references and index. | Audience: Ages: 5-8. | Audience: Grades: K to Grade 3.
Identifiers: LCCN 2016035453 (print) | LCCN 2016036357 (ebook) | ISBN 9781626175976 (hardcover : alk. paper) | ISBN 9781681033273 (ebook)
Subjects: LCSH: Ramadan–Juvenile literature.
Classification: LCC BP186.4 .K58 2017 (print) | LCC BP186.4 (ebook) | DDC 297.3/62–dc23
LC record available at https://lccn.loc.gov/2016035453

Editor: Christina Leaf   Designer: Lois Stanfield

Printed in the United States of America, North Mankato, MN.

Table of Contents

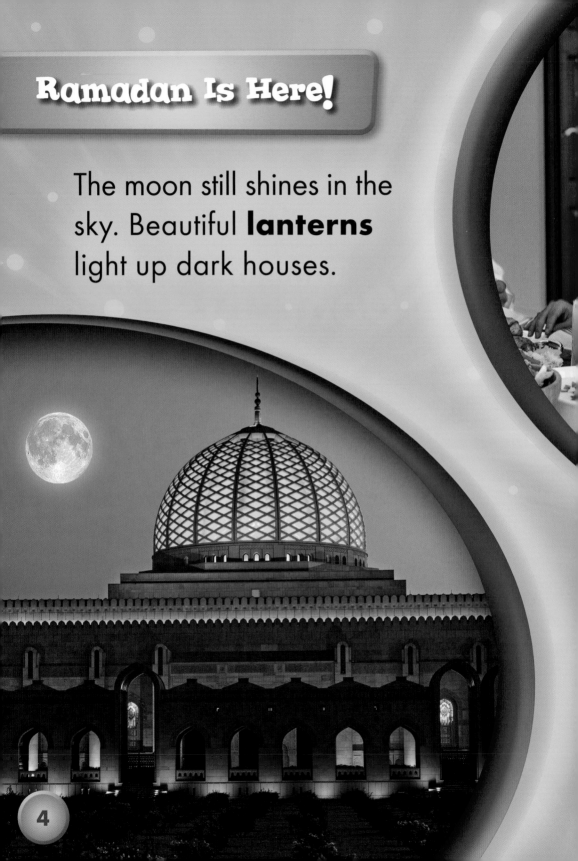

Ramadan Is Here!

The moon still shines in the sky. Beautiful **lanterns** light up dark houses.

Families gather to eat before
the sun rises. They will not eat
or drink again until sundown.
Ramadan is here!

Ramadan is the ninth month of the **Islamic** calendar.

The month is considered holy. People **fast** during the month to honor it.

How Do You Say?

Word	Pronunciation
Allah	al-LAH
Eid al-Fitr	EED ul-FIT-er
Eid Mubarak	EED moo-BAR-ack
Islam	is-LAHM
Muslim	MUHS-lim
Ramadan	rah-mah-DON

Who Celebrates Ramadan?

Muslims around the world celebrate Ramadan. These people follow the messages of the **Prophet** Muhammad.

Healthy Muslims around age 12 and up fast for Ramadan.

Ramadan Beginnings

Qur'an

Muslims believe **Allah** spoke to Muhammad during Ramadan. This happened 1,400 years ago near Mecca.

Muhammad wrote Allah's words down. This became the **Qur'an**. The event made the month holy.

Saudi Arabia

Mecca

Saudi Arabia

N
W E
S

Time to Celebrate

The Islamic calendar follows the moon **phases**. This means Ramadan changes every year.

Ramadan can be in any season.
It lasts about 30 days.

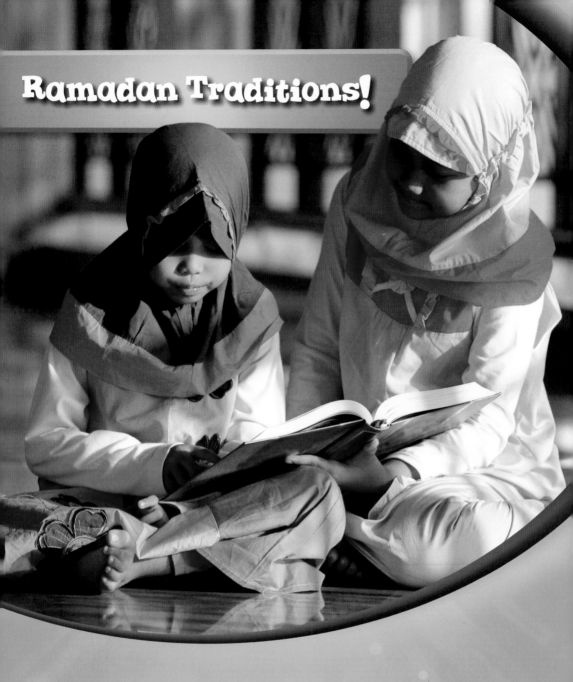

Ramadan Traditions!

The Qur'an tells how to celebrate Ramadan.

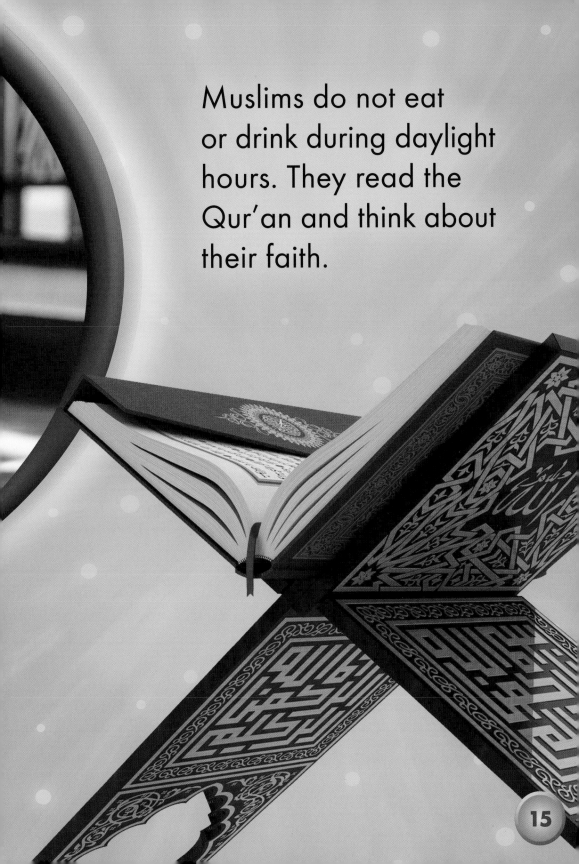

Muslims do not eat or drink during daylight hours. They read the Qur'an and think about their faith.

Prayer is an important part of Ramadan.

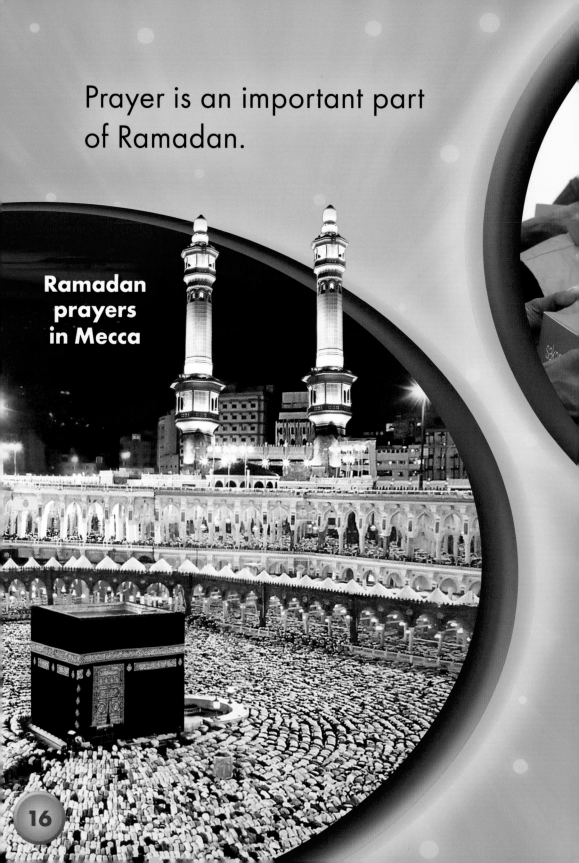

Ramadan prayers in Mecca

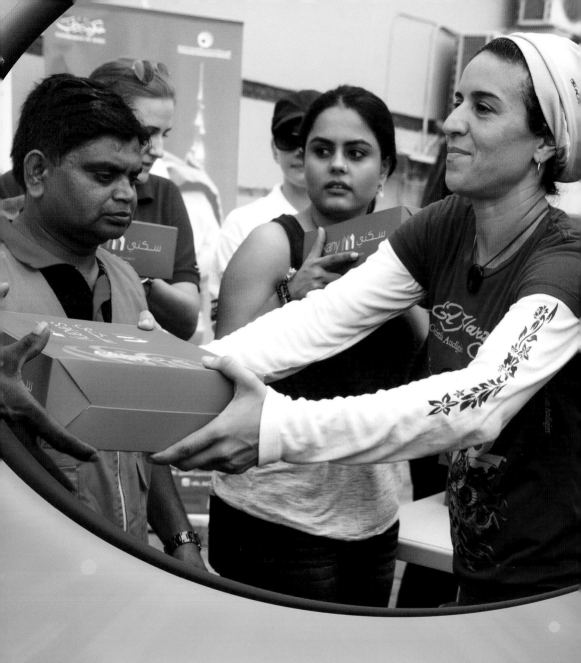

Muslims also **refrain** from bad thoughts, words, and actions. Many give to the poor.

iftar

During Ramadan, Muslims eat a filling meal each morning. The meal after sundown is *iftar*. Muslims often enjoy iftar with friends.

Pineapple Coconut Smoothie

Many Muslims start their day or break their fast in the evening with a healthy fruit smoothie.

Recipe

What You Need:

- ½ cup coconut milk
- ½ cup chopped pineapple
- 1 banana
- ½ teaspoon grated ginger
- ½ teaspoon shredded coconut
- blender
- measuring cups
- measuring spoons
- grater for ginger

What You Do:

1. With an adult, add all ingredients to the blender.
2. Blend until smooth.
3. Add a little water and blend if it is too thick.

Ramadan ends with the **festival** *Eid al-Fitr*. Families visit friends and share sweets.

They greet one another with
"*Eid Mubarak,*" or blessed Eid.
They celebrate their faith!

Glossary

Allah—the Islamic word for God

fast—to go without food or water

festival—celebration

Islamic—related to Islam, a religion that follows the teachings of Muhammad as told to him by Allah

lanterns—covered lights that can be hung or carried

Muslims—people of the Islamic faith

phases—the stages of the moon that change the moon's shape

prophet—someone who shares messages from Allah, or God

Qur'an—the holy book of Islam

refrain—to keep from doing something

To Learn More

AT THE LIBRARY

Heiligman, Deborah. *Celebrate Ramadan & Eid al-Fitr*. Washington, D.C.: National Geographic, 2009.

Pirotta, Saviour. *Id-ul-Fitr*. New York, N.Y.: PowerKids Press, 2008.

Whitman, Sylvia. *Under the Ramadan Moon*. New York, N.Y.: AV2 by Weigl, 2013.

ON THE WEB

Learning more about Ramadan is as easy as 1, 2, 3.

1. Go to www.factsurfer.com.

2. Enter "Ramadan" into the search box.

3. Click the "Surf" button and you will see a list of related web sites.

With factsurfer.com, finding more information is just a click away.

Index

The images in this book are reproduced through the courtesy of: clicksahead, front cover; Ivan Pavlov, p. 4; Owen Price, pp. 4-5; bayualam, pp. 6-7; Saikat Paul, p. 8; Lissma, pp. 8-9; elvirchik abdrahmanova, pp. 10-11; Mehmet Cetin, p. 12; arapix, pp. 12-13; Yamtono_Sardi, pp. 14-15; saffetucuncu, p. 15; prmustafa, p. 16; Kertu, pp. 16-17; Deepak Dogra/ Alamy, p. 18; tvirbickis, p. 19; Hindustan Times/ Newscom, p. 20; Muhammad Hamed/ Zuma Press, pp. 20-21; Helen Lane, p. 22.